BIBL

To:

____

From:

____

Date:

____

Thomas Nelson, Inc.
Nashville

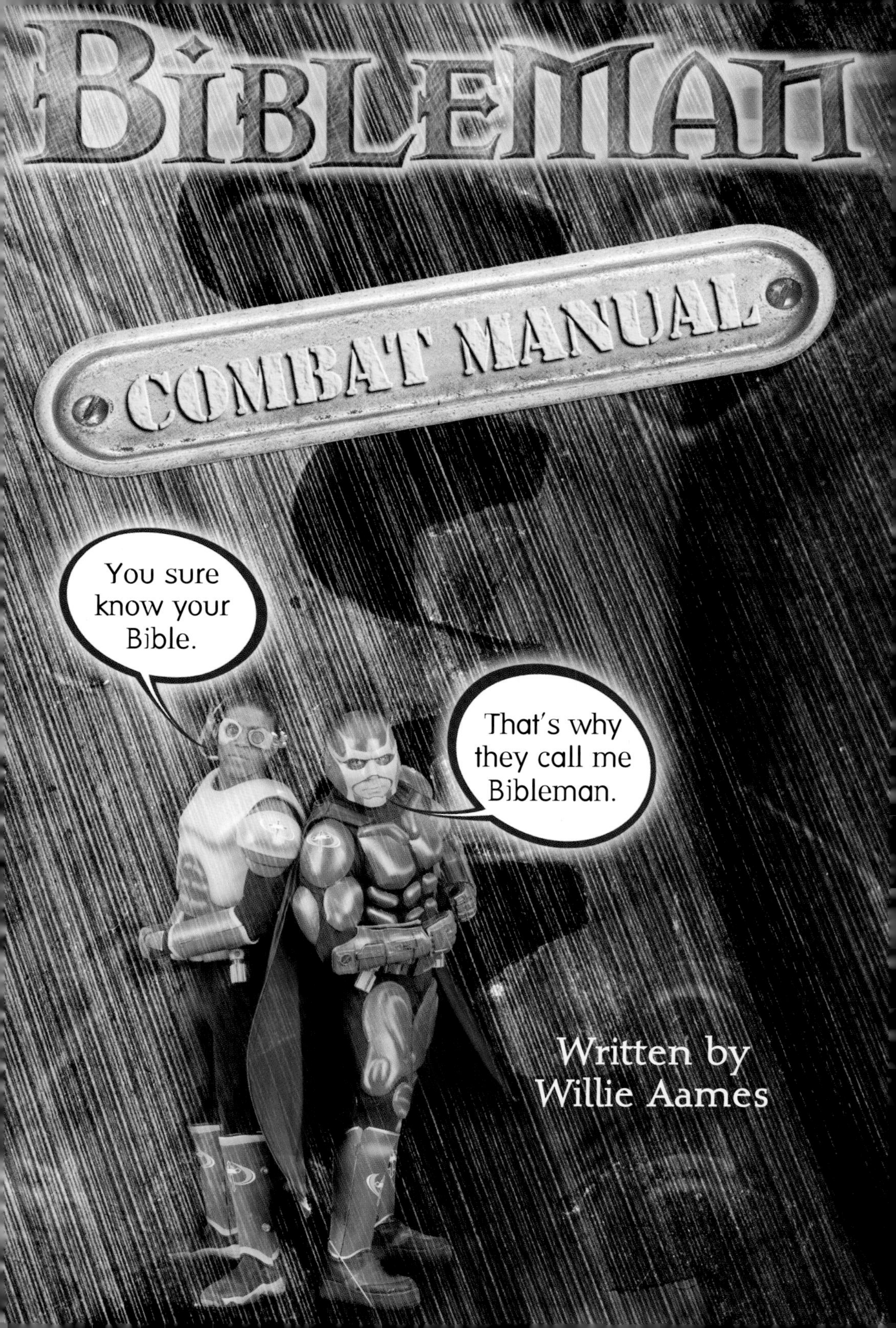
BIBLEMAN
COMBAT MANUAL
You sure know your Bible.
That's why they call me Bibleman.
Written by Willie Aames

TABLE OF CONTENTS

Published in Nashville, Tennessee, by Tommy Nelson®,
a division of Thomas Nelson, Inc.

Creative development: Robin Crouch
Design and production by Lookout Design Group, Inc.

ISBN 0-8499-7716-9

A NOTE FROM WILLIE AAMES ABOUT THE BIBLEMAN MINISTRY

Although Bibleman is a "superhero" character, the main thrust of our ministry is always and will always be evangelical. In all Bibleman videos, books, and even live shows throughout North America, our message is to encourage kids to form a personal relationship with Jesus Christ. God has used our ministry in the past to change the lives of children, and we hope and pray that He continues to bless our work.

Nothing is more precious than the privilege of serving the Lord Jesus Christ. Therefore, our commitment is to the infallible Word of God—*The Holy Bible*. The responsibility we bear in carrying the message of the Gospel is great and made greater still as we attempt to bring the reality of Jesus Christ as Lord and God to children to help their understanding of his grace, care, and love.

I pray that God will use our mutual efforts to plant seeds in our children that only he may harvest. Thank you for allowing us to be a part of your lives as we serve together.

May the Lord bless you,

Willie Aames

YOUR MISSION

A Bibleman Briefing
(Not to be confused with Bibleman briefs.)

Hi everyone!

Did you know that God can make any one of us superheroes? God promises that he will give us all the strength and power we need to overcome evil and stand for righteousness. He asks that we learn to understand his Word and keep it deep in our hearts.

God doesn't care how old we are, how big or small we are, where we live, or how physically strong we are. If we trust him and go into combat with him as our guide, we can all be superheroes and know victory.

Take your time as you complete your training. Study carefully and practice repeating your lessons when you can. It's okay if you finish quickly or if it takes you a year to complete!

I'm glad you've chosen to go through your training and learn about God's ways with me.

BIBLEMAN

HOW TO BEGIN

Stuff you'll need: one Bible and one dictionary.

The Bible says to "be strong in the Lord and in His mighty power." But, to do that, we need to train ourselves to remember important Scriptures. This will help us stand strong. Always remember that God has provided us with everything we need to become leaders and examples for good.

In your training, you will learn important lessons that will help as you become a part of God's army for peace and kindness. Each day, before we begin training, we need to pray and ask God's blessing, empowerment, and guidance in our task.

God promises in the Bible that we can do all things through Christ who strengthens us. But it also says we need to protect ourselves. Our Bibles tell us how we can do this by "putting on the full armor of God." Putting on the armor of God isn't something we wear, like clothes or an inline skating helmet or your grandma's wig. It means making sure we remember what the Bible teaches us. When we hear God's Word, it gives us an invisible armor—like a secret force field that not even the Devil can break through.

As you train for combat and learn each Scripture, you will be putting on an invisible piece of armor. God wants us to do the best job we can: so it's more important to take your time and learn these lessons well than it is to hurry through. When we put on the armor of God, we can be sure that "no weapon formed against us will defeat us."

Good luck!

GET GEARED UP!

As you train for combat, you will be instructed to use the following armaments in addition to the full armor of God.

CRANIAL-CARDIO PASSIVE PROTECTION ARRAY

A collection of attitudes that enable us to keep a peaceful heart and mind.

Sometimes our enemies want us to get confused or mad so we will make mistakes that can get us into trouble. Open your Bible to Philippians 4:4-7. Try to memorize as many of these verses as you can. The next time someone tries to make you mad, calmly recite the whole scripture and then say: "Might I suggest a mutual, in-depth study on this in the original Aramaic or Greek?"

GLOBAL SITUATION FIELD MANUAL

The Holy Bible: the ultimate Combat Manual

Your Bible—otherwise known as your Global Situation Field Manual—holds the answer for all situations. Whenever you find yourself in a combat situation, this Manual will give you the best strategy for victory. It will help you overcome every obstacle and provide protection in every circumstance. It will not, however, protect you from stinky socks!

OPTICAL STEALTH AWARENESS TECHNOLOGIES

Recognizing danger before it happens is one of our best defenses.

Many times our friends try to talk us into doing something we know is wrong or bad. Sometimes we even talk ourselves into doing something wrong! As a combat trainee, you can use special stealth awareness and go on the offensive. Read Philippians 2:5–11 in your Bible. This will help you to see through darkness and guide you.

Situational Example:

Mom tells you to empty the trash.

Mischievous friend says, "Let's play instead."

Optical Stealth Awareness kicks in.

You imagine Mom really, really mad!

And you think to yourself: *No way am I going to play now! I want to live to see my next birthday!*

So you empty the trash.

Preparing for battle is serious business. You must be well rested and lint-free*. And keep a complete collection of combat survival gear on hand in case of emergency.

TACTICAL REINFORCEMENTS

Friends in Christ

The Bible reminds us that fellowship with other Christians is important. They can remind us of our mission and give us strength. Other Christians can also help us when we feel outnumbered. They remind us that we are not alone. (Special tactical note: And it's more fun to eat Popsicles with someone else.)

* If you are linty, you may counteract this by eating a PB&J sandwich.

WHY GET READY FOR BATTLE?

Our fight is not against people on earth. We are fighting against rulers and authorities and powers of this world's darkness.

—EPHESIANS 6:12A

COPY OVER THIS BIBLE VERSE:

Our fight is not against
rulers and authorities and
powers of this worlds
darkness
– Ephesians 6:12a
9/17/01

Bibleman says:

Wearing our armor and using the sword of the Spirit is not about battling other people—it's about having strong hearts and strong minds, always thinking, "what would Jesus do?" We stand for what is good, right, and kind, no matter where we are.

CHAPTER 1 TRUTH

So stand strong,
with the
belt of truth
tied around
your waist.

—EPHESIANS 6:14A

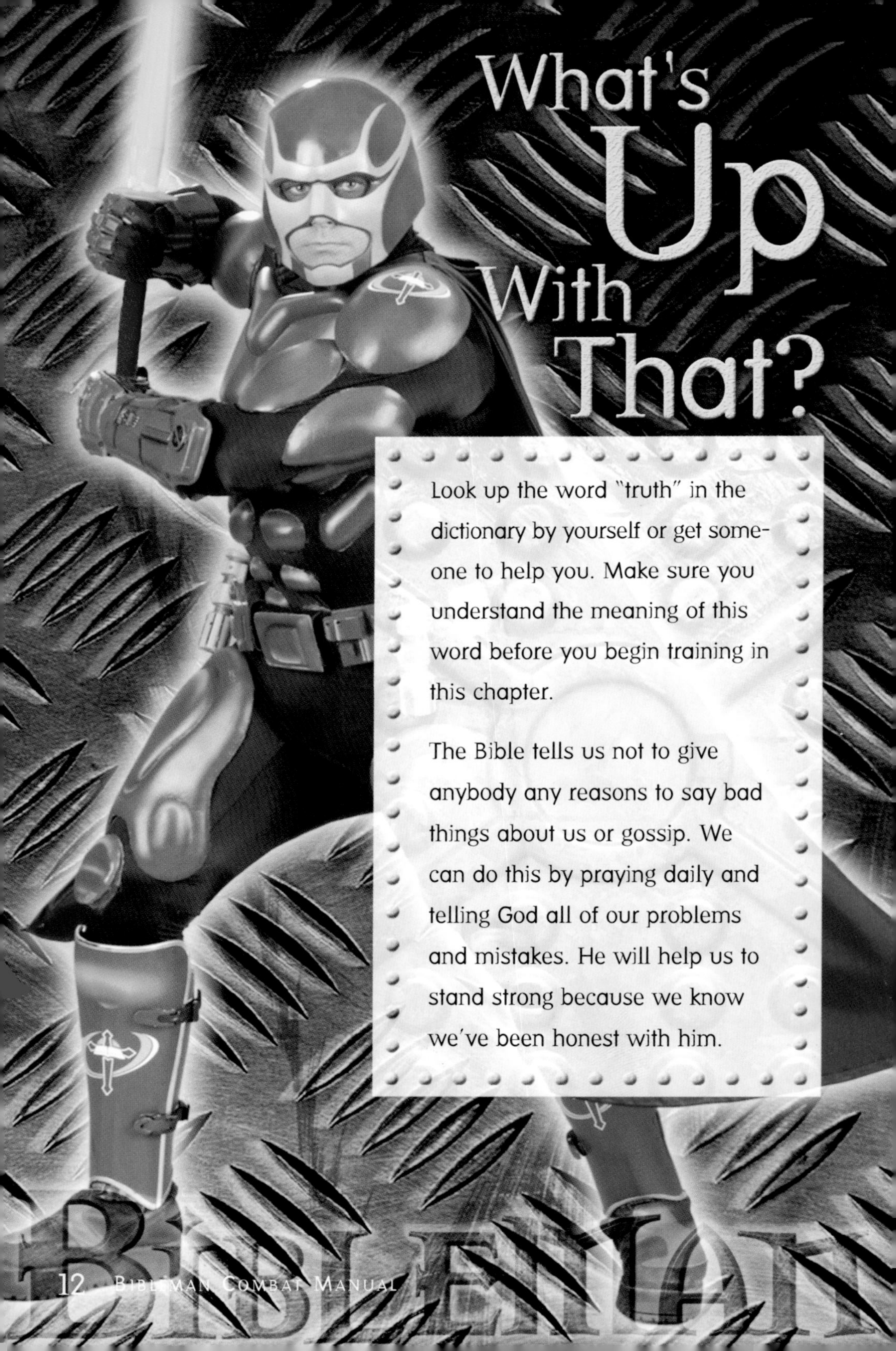

What's Up With That?

Look up the word "truth" in the dictionary by yourself or get someone to help you. Make sure you understand the meaning of this word before you begin training in this chapter.

The Bible tells us not to give anybody any reasons to say bad things about us or gossip. We can do this by praying daily and telling God all of our problems and mistakes. He will help us to stand strong because we know we've been honest with him.

HE'S THE MAN

Jesus answered, "I am the way. And I am the truth and the life. The only way to the Father is through me."

—John 14:6

Copy over this Bible verse:

Jesus answered, "I am the way. And I am the truth and the life. The only way to the Father is through me."

— John 14:16

9/18/01

Bibleman says:

Jesus tells us that all truth comes from him and God's Word in the Bible. Because the Bible is God's way of teaching us truth, it's important that we learn as much about it as possible.

THINK ABOUT IT!

Brothers and sisters, continue to think about the things that are good and worthy of praise.

—Philippians 4:8a

COPY OVER THIS BIBLE VERSE:

____

____

____

____

____

____

____

Bibleman says:

Sometimes we know we're going to get in trouble for something we did. (Or didn't do!) And bad thoughts can happen—like thinking of a lie to tell. If that ever happens to you, remember this verse. God always knows what we think. He wants our ideas to make him proud of us!

CODE RED

Time to gear up!

Global Situation Field Manual (The Holy Bible)

Anything that contradicts what God says in the Bible can be considered untruthful. If you don't have your Field Manual ready, move forward with tactical reinforcements. Call a fellow friend in Christ and ask for advice on this tactical situation. If that doesn't work, call your mom.

Cranial-Cardio Passive Protection Array:

Whenever you feel you're going into combat, adopt a peaceful heart and mind. This allows you to think clearly and stand strong.

Bibleman Tactical Hint:

If you're alone and surrounded: This is where our combat training really kicks in. If you find yourself in situations where others are not being truthful, you must call upon our commander-in-chief, Jesus, in your heart and your mind. Ask for strength. Then, even though you are surrounded and outnumbered, God will provide a way for you to escape. Never be afraid to stand strong.

THERE WILL BE TROUBLE

"In this world you will have trouble. But be brave! I have defeated the world!"

—John 16:33b

Copy over this Bible verse:

Bibleman says:

There will always be temptations to do the wrong thing. But Jesus says that, through the truth of his Word, he will help you overcome these temptations. So when you find yourself in trouble and tempted to go against truth, remember this verse. Be brave and remember that Jesus has already defeated temptation. This will help you choose the right path.

MY BATTLE FOR TRUTH

Write down one of your troubles and how you won by wearing the waistbelt of truth.

NOTHING TO HIDE

". . . you will know the truth. And the truth will make you free."

—JOHN 8:32

COPY OVER THIS BIBLE VERSE:

Bibleman says:

Jesus said that, through his teachings, you would know the truth and that it would set you free. Being truthful means that we have nothing to hide. And because we have nothing to hide, we are free to be who we are, no matter who we're with or where we are.

TRUTH=FREEDOM

Was there ever a time when something happened, and you told the truth? When you wanted nothing to hide? How did you feel inside? This is the kind of freedom that Jesus gives us! In the spaces below, describe a time you told the truth and it set you free!

THINGS THAT ARE TRUE

Think about the things that are true and honorable and right and pure and beautiful and respected.

—PHILIPPIANS 4:8B

Write this verse in the spaces below. Think about what you've been learning about truth in this chapter. After writing down this verse, practice saying it aloud until you remember it.

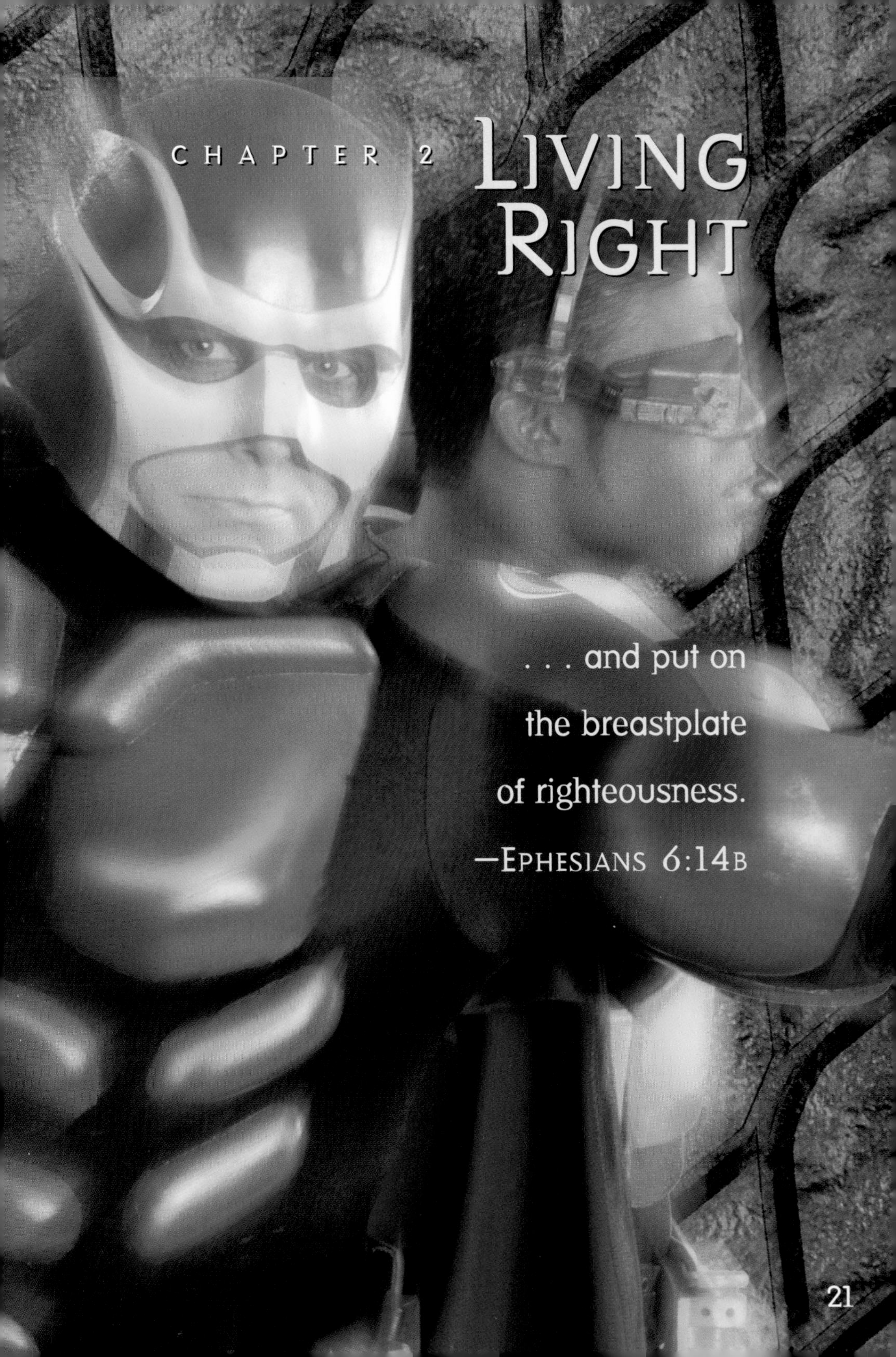

CHAPTER 2

LIVING RIGHT

. . . and put on
the breastplate
of righteousness.
—EPHESIANS 6:14B

What's Up With That?

Look up "righteousness" in the dictionary or get someone to help you look it up. Living right means practicing righteousness. Try to understand the meanings of righteousness as you work through this chapter.

Wearing the breastplate of righteousness means living our lives right. It doesn't mean being perfect. It also means that—in our attitudes and in our hearts—we want to do what is right. Like trying to live our lives according to God's will. This is all that Jesus expects from us, and he will do the rest.

BIBLEMAN

READ ME FIRST!

My God, I want to do what you want. Your teachings are in my heart.

—PSALM 40:8

COPY OVER THIS BIBLE VERSE:

Bibleman says:

This is one of David's prayers. He was one of the great Bible heroes, and he was also a warrior. God said David was a man after God's own heart.

This is a great prayer to say before you go into combat.

THE BASICS

Bibleman says:

The Ten Commandments are the most important instructions that God ever gave to people before he gave us Jesus. Below each commandment are spaces for you to write them down. Try to memorize them all.

1) You must not have any other gods except me.

____

____

2) You must not make for yourselves any idols.

____

____

3) You must not use the name of the LORD your God thoughtlessly.

____

____

4) Remember to keep the Sabbath as a holy day.

____

____

5) Honor your father and your mother.

____

6) You must not murder anyone.

____

7) You must not be guilty of adultery.

____

____

8) You must not steal.

____

9) You must not tell lies about your neighbor.

____

____

10) You must not want to take your neighbor's house or anything that belongs to your neighbor.

____

____

____

A NEW COMMAND

"I give you a new command: Love each other. You must love each other as I have loved you."

—John 13:34

Copy over this Bible verse:

Bibleman says:

If you are angry or have hate in your heart, you cannot go into combat God's way. So he has given us a new command to love each other like he loves us.

CODE RED

Righteousness is about trying to do the best job you can. If you're being tempted or distracted from doing your best job, you need to gear up.

Optical Stealth Awareness Technologies:

Try to recognize that you're being lured away from your primary goal. Notice the affect it will have on your position as a leader for Christ.

As always, go back to the Field Manual. Proverbs 27:12 says:

When a wise person sees
danger ahead, he avoids it.
But a foolish person keeps going
and gets into trouble.

Bibleman Tactical Hint:

When in doubt, leave it out. If you're not sure of something, don't move forward without speaking to an adult or your pastor.

KEEP TRYING

Take a moment, and think about all of the jobs you tried to do in the past. This is one of the best ways to see if you're living a righteous life. Did you complete those jobs on time? Did you do them with a cheerful heart? Did you do them to the best of your ability? If yes—congratulations—you're well on your way. If not, don't worry. Jesus wants you to keep trying.

Now, in the space below, describe a time when you chose to do something in a righteous manner.

SERVE HIM

As for me and my family, we will serve the Lord.

—Joshua 24:15f

Copy over this Bible verse:

Bibleman says:

This verse shows a great example of someone who wants to live a righteous life and won't be bullied or pressured into changing his mind.

MY OWN BATTLE

In your own words, give three or four examples of how you can battle unrighteousness. Use examples from home, school, or anywhere.

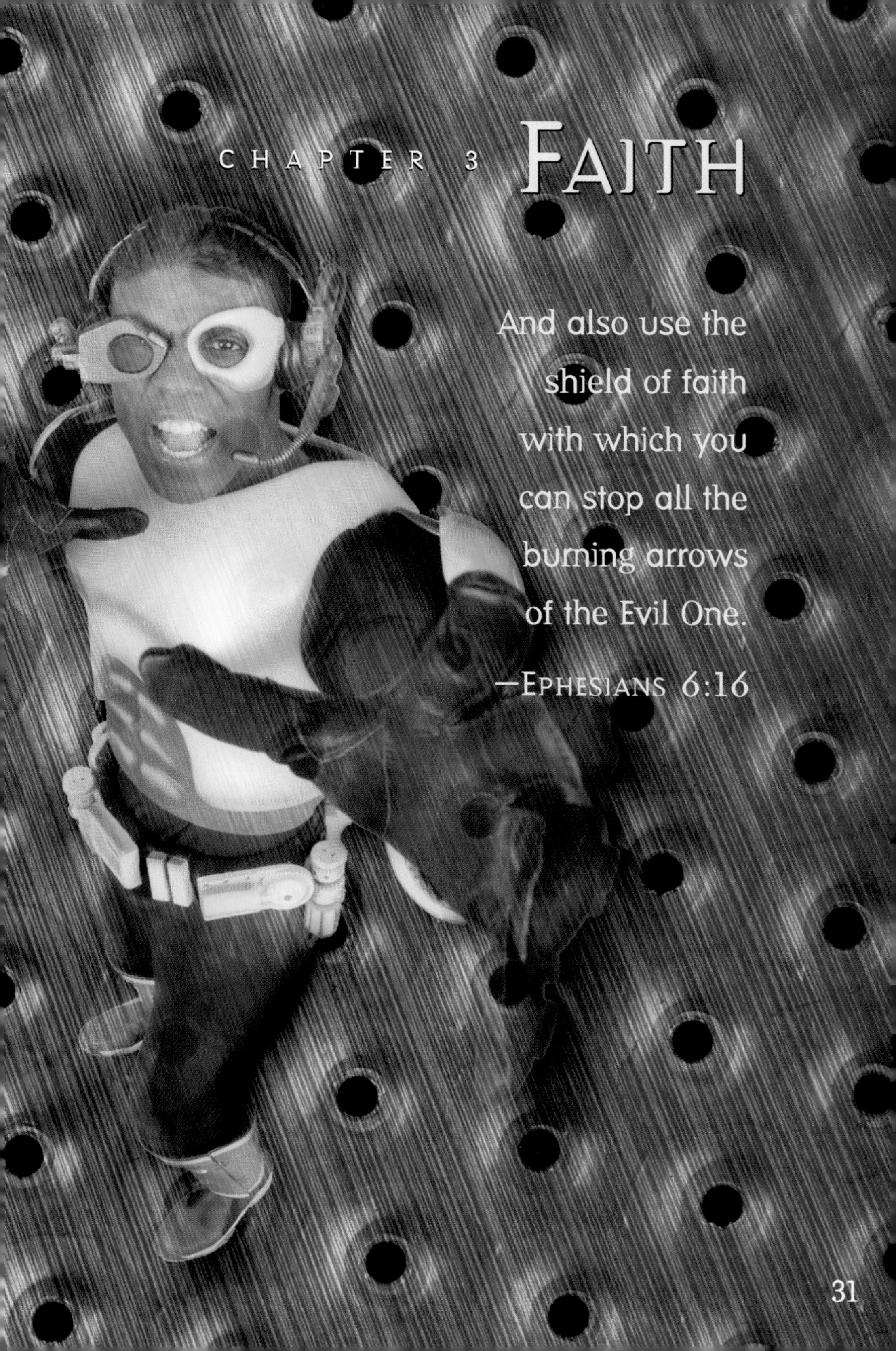

CHAPTER 3 FAITH

And also use the shield of faith with which you can stop all the burning arrows of the Evil One.

—Ephesians 6:16

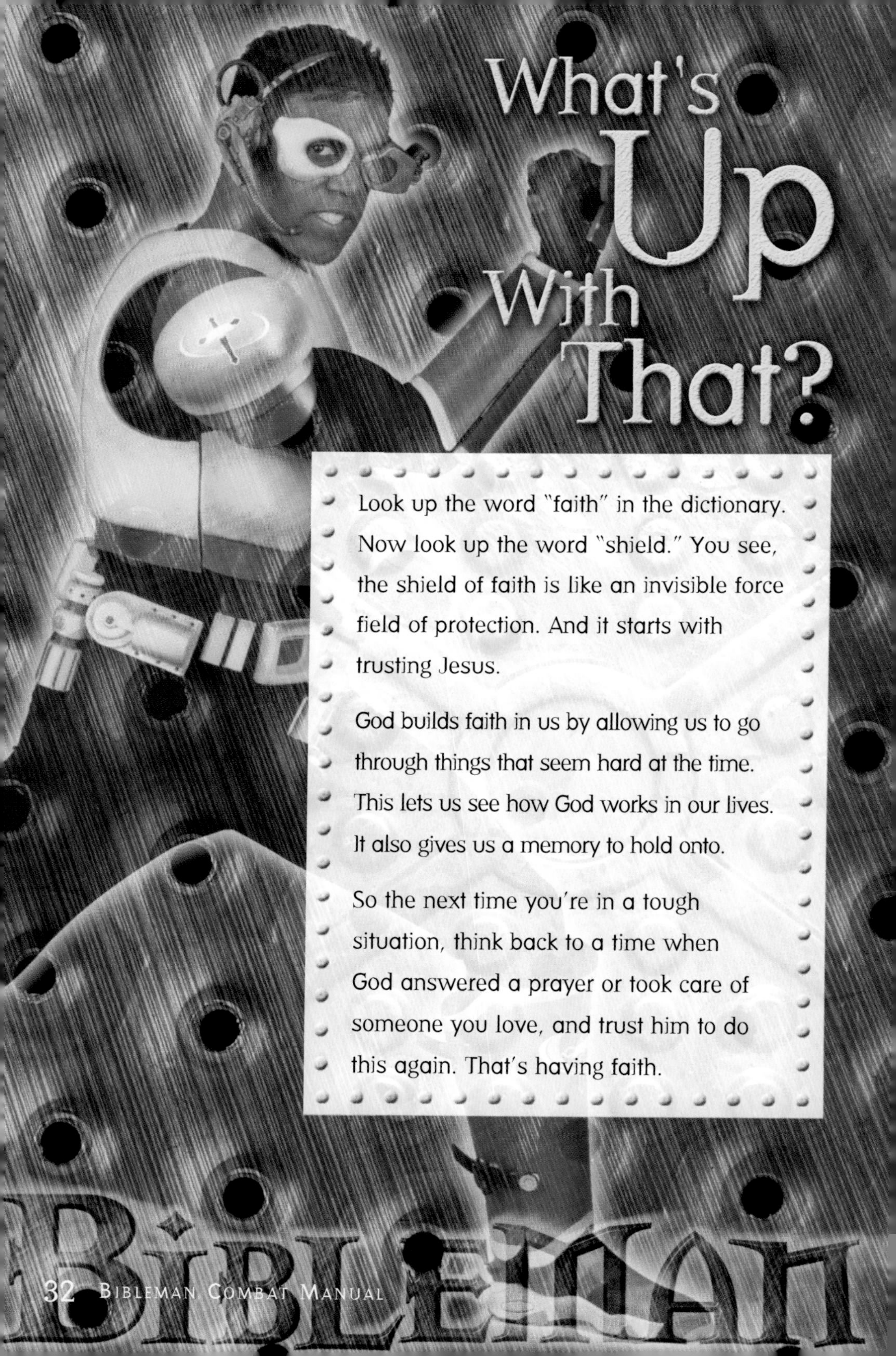

What's Up With That?

Look up the word "faith" in the dictionary. Now look up the word "shield." You see, the shield of faith is like an invisible force field of protection. And it starts with trusting Jesus.

God builds faith in us by allowing us to go through things that seem hard at the time. This lets us see how God works in our lives. It also gives us a memory to hold onto.

So the next time you're in a tough situation, think back to a time when God answered a prayer or took care of someone you love, and trust him to do this again. That's having faith.

TRUST THE COMMANDER

Trust the Lord with all your heart.
Don't depend on your own understanding.
Remember the Lord in everything you do.
And he will give you success.

—Proverbs 3:5-6

Bibleman says:

Sometimes having faith seems like the hardest thing of all. Understanding God's ways can be a challenge. But don't worry. We're in good company. Some of the greatest heroes of the Bible questioned their own faith before realizing that God would never let them down.

CODE RED

Time to gear up!

Tactical reinforcements:

Whenever you feel weakened or your faith threatened, tactical reinforcements are a must. Get together with your parents, your pastor, or other Christian friends. Describe to them the ways the enemy is trying to weaken your faith. You'll find that these friends in Christ help strengthen you. They may know something that can help. And their prayers for you will help build your strength in combat. By bringing in your tactical reinforcements, you will discover that you're not the only one who's been attacked in this way. It happens to everyone. Even Bibleman.

PRAYER HELPS

Write about a time when God strengthened your faith by answering a prayer.

I DON'T UNDERSTAND

The Lord says:
My thoughts and my ways
are not like yours.

—Isaiah 55:8

Bibleman says:

God tells us that sometimes we won't understand why or how he accomplishes goals. But a big part of faith is trusting him to keep his promises.

Many important people in the Bible didn't understand why God wanted them to do certain things. But they did them anyway and later found out what was God's plan.

Copy this verse over in the spaces below to help you memorize it.

____

____

____

____

____

BATTLE DOUBT WITH FAITH

Write about a time when it seemed that God wasn't answering your prayers. Were you able to stay faithful? Write about that, too.

ENJOYING YOUR FAITH

But let all those who worship you rejoice and be glad.

—Psalm 70:4

Copy over this Bible verse:

____

____

____

____

____

____

Bibleman says:

Having faith gives us the freedom to live without fear or worry. And it also gives us a reason to rejoice! Rejoice means to let your joy out. Show others how much you enjoy having faith in the Lord. And be glad that you have faith!

SHARE IT!

Sharing faith with other people happens in many, many ways. Sometimes it's just a smile, a friendly attitude, or a willingness to care. What are the ways you share your faith with others? Write them down.

STRENGTHEN YOUR FAITH

Here are two ways to strengthen your faith. Write down some other ways that will help make your faith stronger. You don't have to fill this all out at once. Come back later and write down more ideas as you discover them!

Prayer

Fellowship

CHAPTER 4

SALVATION

Accept God's
salvation to be
your helmet.
—EPHESIANS 6:17A

What's Up With That?

The helmet is one of the most important pieces of armor because it protects our minds and our thoughts while in combat.

Look up the word "salvation" in the dictionary. Salvation means that God has given us his special protection. No matter what happens, he will always be with us. Salvation gives us hope. And without hope, no battle can be won.

BIBLEMAN

HE'S THE ROCK, TOO!

He is my rock and my salvation.
He is my defender;
I will not be defeated.

—PSALM 62:6

COPY OVER THIS BIBLE VERSE:

____

____

____

____

____

____

Bibleman says:

The Bible says that the Lord is our rock and our salvation. That means that he is strong and true. And he is there to protect us. God wants us to know that he will defend us in battle. So we already know we've won!

ONE SON, ONE WAY

"I am the way, and the truth, and the life. The only way to the Father is through me."

—JOHN 14:6

COPY OVER THIS BIBLE VERSE:

____

____

____

____

____

____

Bibleman says:

This may be the most important verse in the entire Bible. It tells us that Jesus Christ is truly the Son of God, died for our sins, rose again, and is alive today. Many people believe that if they're just good people, then they can get into heaven. But Jesus said that unless we have a relationship with him, love him, and carry him in our hearts, we cannot get to heaven.

WE ALL MAKE MISTAKES

All people have sinned and are not good enough for God's glory . . .

—ROMANS 3:23

COPY OVER THIS BIBLE VERSE:

Bibleman says:

Sin is a word we use to describe the things we do that do not please God. God wants to erase sin from everyone's life. You could think of your relationship with Jesus as a giant eraser that takes away all of the bad or unpleasant things you've ever done. This is what God wants for us.

WALK AWAY FROM SIN

But if we confess our sins, he will forgive our sins, because we can trust God to do what is right. He will cleanse us from all the wrongs we have done.

—1 JOHN 1:9

COPY OVER THIS BIBLE VERSE:

____

____

____

____

____

____

Bibleman says:

As a part of our combat training, we must learn to walk away from sin before it happens. But sometimes, if we've already sinned, we need to tell God that we are sorry. This kind of apology is called "confessing" our sins. If we are doing something that we know is wrong, and we stop and walk away from it, this is what the Bible calls "repenting."

REPENT AND BE HAPPY

Write about a time when you walked away from a sin in your life. How did it make you feel? How do you think it made God feel?

CODE RED

Get out your gear!

Optical Stealth Awareness Technologies:

There are many forms of stealth awareness. Sometimes little alarms go off in our heads before we do something wrong—and we stop, listen, and avoid danger. Other times, when we hear the alarms, we choose to be bold and stumble into a bad situation. Recognize when you are doing something that would not be pleasing to God.

Another form of stealth awareness is the hardest to deploy. That's recognizing that you've done something wrong when you don't want to admit it. No matter what stage you're in, there's good news. God forgives you. He forgives for thinking about it, for thinking about doing it, and for doing it.

Cranial-Cardio Passive Protection Array:

Check your heart and attitude. Are you worried? Does your heart ache? Are you unhappy? If you feel any of these things, call in tactical reinforcements.

Tactical Reinforcements:

Being able to talk to other Christians about the sin in our lives helps us to let it go. It strengthens us so we can walk away. Our friends in Christ encourage us as we move through the battlefield. After calling in Tactical Reinforcements, it is imperative that you consult the Global Field Situation Manual for concrete advice, instruction, and healing.

I BELIEVE

If someone says, "I believe that Jesus is the Son of God," then God lives in him. And he lives in God.

—1 John 4:15

Copy over this Bible verse:

Bibleman says:

Believing that Jesus is God's Son is the first step to salvation. Doesn't it feel good to know that God lives in you—and that you live in him? Now that's Good News that makes me feel very peaceful!

DON'T GIVE UP

We must not become tired of doing good. We will receive our harvest of eternal life at the right time if we do not give up.

—GALATIANS 6:9

COPY OVER THIS BIBLE VERSE:

____

____

____

____

____

____

Bibleman says:

God promises us that we can live forever with him in heaven through salvation. But it's important to remember that he wants us to do good things here on the planet. Let yourself get excited about doing good! And then you'll never "become tired" of it.

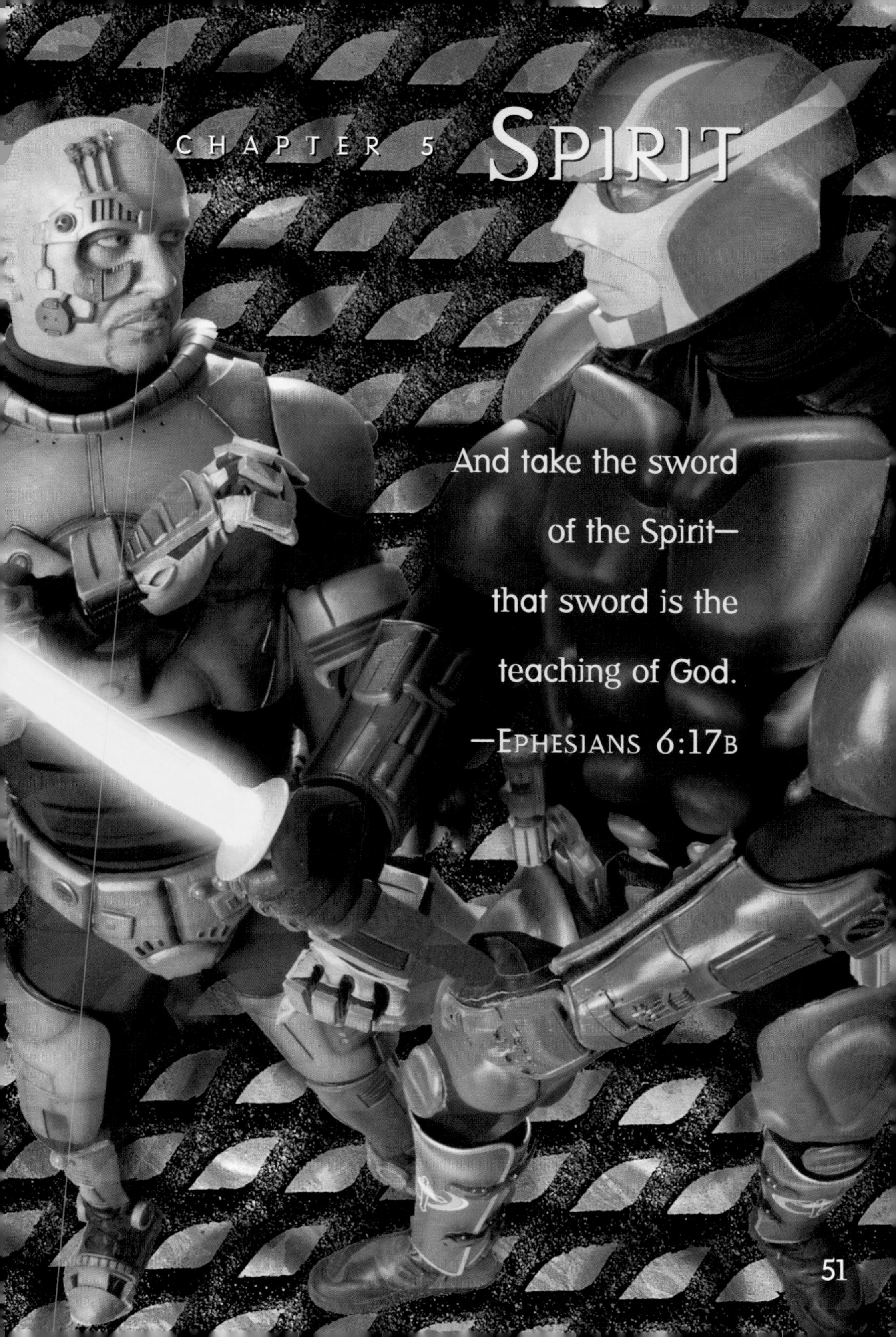

CHAPTER 5 SPIRIT

And take the sword
of the Spirit—
that sword is the
teaching of God.
—EPHESIANS 6:17B

What's Up With That?

The Bible says that God's Word is sharper than a two-edged sword. It helps us tell the difference between right and wrong in spiritual matters. It's called the sword of the spirit because it divides good and evil. Just like a knife separates one half of a PB&J sandwich from the other.

FOLLOW THE LIGHT

Your word is like a lamp for my feet and a light for my path.

—Psalm 119:105

COPY OVER THIS BIBLE VERSE:

____

____

____

____

____

____

Bibleman says:

This verse means that God's Word will always light the way for us. Take time to read the Bible when you don't know which way to turn. God's Word can shed light on even the darkest situation.

WORDS OF WISDOM

Did you know Proverbs is the book of wisdom? This means reading Proverbs can help you make smart decisions on the battlefield. Here's an idea you can try! There are about thirty-one days in each month. And there are thirty-one Proverbs. Try reading one a day for a month.

Write your favorite Proverb in the spaces below.

____

____

____

____

____

____

____

Bibleman says:

My favorite Proverb is 19:2!

CODE RED

Whoops!

When we're out of practice reading God's Word, bad things can happen. It's time to gear up!

Global Field Manual:

Start with a favorite verse.

Optical Stealth Awareness Technologies:

Recognize that being out of the Word of God is a dangerous path.

Cranial-Cardio Passive Protection Array:

You might find yourself angry, upset, confused, or just plain old stinky. Code Red! This is a sign that your stinkiness could grow. To avoid supreme stinkiness, you must proceed directly into the Word. Tactical reinforcements are not necessary but helpful, depending on the extent of contamination (or stinkiness).

IN A WORD

In the beginning there was the Word. The Word was with God, and the Word was God. He was with God in the beginning.

—JOHN 1:1-2

COPY OVER THIS BIBLE VERSE:

Bibleman says:

In the Bible, when someone mentions "the Word," they are usually talking about the Son of God, Jesus Christ. So when the Bible says the Word was with God, it's talking about Jesus, because in the beginning, God and Jesus were together. Today, the Word also means the books of the Holy Bible.

FROM NOW ON

But the word of the Lord will live forever.

—1 PETER 1:25

COPY OVER THIS BIBLE VERSE:

Bibleman says:

Everything God promises will always be true and never change. We can count on him now, and a hundred katrillion, kabillion, kazillion years from now. And definitely until high school.

LIVING THE WORD

I write to you, young people, because you are strong; the teaching of God lives in you, and you have defeated the Evil One.

—1 JOHN 2:14

COPY OVER THIS BIBLE VERSE:

____

____

____

____

____

____

Bibleman says:

The Bible tells that we have already defeated evil when God's teaching lives in us. This means that if we train hard in the Word, then it will become a part of us. But remember—even though we are strong, it's not our power that defeats evil, but the power of Jesus Christ living in us.

MY PRAYER

Write down a prayer for yourself, asking God to help you make time to read his Word. It's also important to ask for guidance and understanding while you read God's Word.

Dear God,

____

____

____

____

____

____

____

____

____

____ Amen.

HEAR AND OBEY

Jesus said . . . "happy are those who hear the teaching of God and obey it."

—Luke 11:28

Copy over this Bible verse:

____

____

____

____

____

____

Bibleman says:

Did you know the Bible can make you happy? That's what Jesus says. And since he is the Word, he ought to know about the Word. So try it—see how much you can learn and obey, then notice how happy it makes you!

CHAPTER 6 PEACE

And on your feet wear the Good News of peace to help you stand strong.

—EPHESIANS 6:15

What's Up With That?

The Bible says the Good News is that Jesus died for us on the cross, was buried, and came back to life. Because he did these things for us, we can be saved. That is good news! We can be saved from the consequences of everything we've done wrong.

Actually, you don't wear the Good News on your feet—this is one place God wants you to put your feet in your mouth. Paul wrote the armor of God sequence like a description of the armor a Roman soldier wore. And he used "shoes" because he wanted us to spread the Good News wherever we go. Today we would probably call them the inline roller blades of peace.

BIBLEMAN

HE CAME IN PEACE

This is the beginning of the Good News about Jesus Christ, the Son of God, as the prophet Isaiah wrote: "I will send my messenger ahead of you, who will prepare your way."

—MARK 1:1-2

COPY OVER THIS BIBLE VERSE:

____

____

____

____

____

____

____

Bibleman says:

Hundreds of years before Jesus came, people already knew that He was coming. They waited for the Son of God to come, so he could prepare our way to heaven.

PRACTICE PEACE

Then Jesus said again, "Peace be with you! As the Father sent me, I now send you."

—John 20:21

Copy over this Bible verse:

____

____

____

____

____

Bibleman says:

There are interesting ways to practice peace. Like, when friends want to leave someone else out of an activity or party or game. Be the one that stands for peace. Try to get everyone to agree to give the other person a chance. Practicing peace doesn't always mean "going along with the crowd". You may get some weird looks at first. But tell your group that if they were being left out, you would stick up for them too. Then maybe they'll understand and change their minds. And then you will have been a warrior for peace!

PRAYER FOR PEACE

The Bible says we are to pray continually, which means all the time. We're even supposed to pray for our enemies! So if you have an argument with someone, God wants you to pray that your enemy will be okay.

God is so interested in our prayers that he wants us to pray for peace everywhere, in our homes, our hearts, for our friends, our president and country, our schools. We can pray for peace everywhere.

Write down your own prayer for peace and include someone you know that needs peace right now.

____

____

____

____

____

Bibleman says:

The Bible also asks that we pray for the peace of Jerusalem and Israel. If you can remember, try to include them too!

CODE RED

It's amazing that even though Jesus is God and can do anything he wants, he chooses to be the one who refuses to fight. He only wants to do what is right and peaceful. When he was on earth, other people tried to get him to fight. But he didn't. Even when he was about to be taken away by Roman soldiers, and Peter pulled out a sword to fight them, Jesus told him to put it away!

If you find yourself in a situation that threatens the peace in your heart, or the peace among you and your friends you may need help. **GEAR UP!**

Cranial-Cardio Passive Protection Array:

Try to recognize that something is going on around you that may end up with someone's feelings getting hurt, or worse! Stay calm. Remind others that "this would not be what God would want from us".

Tactical Reinforcements:

In extreme circumstances, the wise move may be to leave the area and get the help of an adult. This is bringing in "the big guns" of tactical reinforcements.

Bibleman Tactical Hint:

Never stay where you are sure it may get dangerous—no matter what others tell you. Even the apostle Paul knew when it was time to "boogie on out" so he could be used by God in another way. This isn't running away—it's called being smart!

Bibleman says:

Take some time to make up tactical situations with your friends or family. Take turns pretending that you are being attacked or are in a dangerous situation. What armor will you use? What will you say? Each person should imagine and say out loud his or her plan for peace in the situation. You can write down the best ideas:

PEACE BE WITH YOU

I go to bed and sleep in peace. Lord, only you keep me safe.

—PSALM 4:8

COPY OVER THIS BIBLE VERSE:

____

____

____

____

____

Bibleman says:

So you've learned that God wants us to spread the Good News of peace. Also know that he wants us to feel this peace ourselves. When it's time to go to bed at night, remember this: The Lord is keeping you safe. Show how thankful you are by going to bed in peace. (This means being nice to those around you. And brushing your teeth!)

HOW I SPREAD PEACE

You have studied many ways to help spread peace: through prayer, being a friend, and walking away from a situation. In the space below, write other ways to help spread peace.

ON THE FRONT LINE

Christ himself is our peace.

—EPHESIANS 2:14

COPY OVER THIS BIBLE VERSE:

Bibleman says:

It is much harder to be a warrior for peace than it is to fight back in anger. Try to remember that Christ is your peace. And since he lives in you, so does peace. If something is happening that makes you feel far away from the peace of Jesus—it's not of God! So turn away if you can't spread peace on that battlefront. We are always on the front line if we love Jesus and want to obey him.

CHAPTER 7 VICTORY

Finally, be strong
in the Lord and in his
great power. Wear the
full armor of God.
Wear God's armor so that
you can fight against the
devil's evil tricks.

—EPHESIANS 6:10

What's Up With That?

Even though The Bible says that we will have victory, there will always be many battles we have to fight.

Try not to think of Victory as the "end" of our troubles. Each victory we have over any sin in our lives may come back and try to take that victory away again, so we must always stand strong and use what we have learned to keep having victory after victory.

DON'T WORRY! Sometimes we make mistakes and we lose the small battles temporarily. But it's only for the moment! That's when we go to our Commander in Chief Jesus, and he allows us to start over again fresh and new.

BIBLEMAN

ALWAYS BE READY!

Pray in the Spirit at all times with all kinds of prayers, asking for everything you need. To do this you must always be ready and never give up.

—EPHESIANS 6:18

COPY OVER THIS BIBLE VERSE:

Bibleman says:

Sometimes we forget that Jesus will always give everything we need to have victory over everything! But, we must never give up—even if it seems that we can't win.

GIVE YOURSELF TO GOD

So give yourselves completely to God. Stand against the devil, and the devil will run from you.

—James 4:7

COPY OVER THIS BIBLE VERSE:

Bibleman says:

Way cool! All we have to do is say "no" to the devil's lies and tricks, and he has to leave us alone!

SERVE ONLY HIM

Jesus said to the devil, "Go away from me, Satan! It is written in the Scriptures, 'You must worship the Lord your God and serve only him.'"

—MATTHEW 4:10

COPY OVER THIS BIBLE VERSE:

Bibleman says:

Even just saying this can help us feel stronger. And the more we use this Scripture, the stronger we will feel.

HAVE NO FEAR

Where God's love is, there is no fear, because God's perfect love drives out fear.

—1 JOHN 4:18

COPY OVER THIS BIBLE VERSE:

____

____

____

____

____

____

Bibleman says:

Always remember that the Bible is filled with promises that God keeps. Let your heart be full of God's love, and he will be right there with you. In fact, with his love, he will take away all your fears!

CODE RED

Not experiencing Victory?!

Gear Up!

Use everything in your arsenal on a daily basis! But here is the key: Be patient! One of the hardest things we learn as Christian soldiers is to "sit at Jesus' feet". This means learning and being patient while we learn.

God always waits for us to be ready for victory before he gives it to us. This way, there's time for us pass our knowledge along to someone else. Many people can learn through our example. Patience is one of the most important pieces of battle gear.

LOVE ENEMIES?

"But I say to you, love your enemies. Pray for those who hurt you."

—Matthew 5:44

Copy over this Bible verse:

____

____

____

____

____

____

Bibleman says:

Pray for those who hurt us? Yeah, I know it's hard. But the Bible says in 1 John 4:21 that if you love God you will also love your brother. Even our enemies are our brothers! We can never have victory by pushing people away—even if they are wrong. Pray that Jesus will come into their hearts and give them what he has given us! Talk about victory! We get new friends, and Satan loses hold of another person. Yes! That's true victory!

BUT WAIT, THERE'S MORE

Write a list of people for whom you pray:

____

____

____

____

____

____

____

____

____

Now write the name of at least one person that you think may be your enemy. Try to practice praying for him or her too!

____

NEVER GIVE UP!

Praise be to the God and Father of our Lord Jesus Christ. In God's great mercy he has caused us to be born again into a living hope, because Jesus Christ rose from the dead.

—1 PETER 1:3

COPY OVER THIS BIBLE VERSE:

Remember that Jesus will never give us more than we can handle. Never give up hope. There is always time to have victory. That's the great thing about being a Christian! We can always believe that we will have victory, and we can always start over again until we achieve it!

DRILLS

TRUTH

Do not use your Bible, this Combat Manual, or anything else to help you while completing your Drills. In the spaces below, write down what Jesus said in John 14:6.

LIVING RIGHT

Do not use your Bible, this Combat Manual, or anything else to help you while completing your Drills. In the spaces below, write down what Jesus said in John 13:34

FAITH

Do not use your Bible, this Combat Manual, or anything else to help you while completing your Drills. In the spaces below, write down the words found in Proverbs 3:5-6.

SALVATION

Do not use your Bible, this Combat Manual, or anything else to help you while completing your Drills. In the spaces below, write down the words found in 1 John 4:15.

SPIRIT

Do not use your Bible, this Combat Manual, or anything else to help you while completing your Drills. In the spaces below, write down the words found in 1 John 2:14.

DRILLS

PEACE

Do not use your Bible, this Combat Manual, or anything else to help you while completing your Drills. In the spaces below, write down the words found in Psalm 4:8.

VICTORY

Do not use your Bible, this Combat Manual, or anything else to help you while completing your Drills. In the spaces below, write down the words found in James 4:7.

CONGRATULATIONS!

You have successfully completed basic training for combat! It is important to read and re-read what you've learned in this manual—so that no matter when or where evil lurks, your training will kick in! Return to your Combat Manual often. Soon, you'll automatically know how to gear up and how to do battle until you have victory!

If you've completed this manual, but you don't feel ready to ask Jesus into your heart to become your Lord and Savior—don't worry! Jesus knows when the right time will be. But if you are ready, I want you to tell you parents, your pastor, or the person who gave you this Combat Manual, so that they can speak with you about asking Jesus into your heart right away! If you do, nothing would make Jesus happier! If you're not ready, it's okay!! Jesus still loves you very much! And you can still use this book—and your Bible—as a way to get to know Jesus better.

Stand Strong!

BIBLEMAN

AUTHORIZATION:

Now that you are combat-ready, you're eligible to receive an official Bibleman Combat Manual *graduation certificate! (Tactical Hint: be sure you've successfully completed the Drills section of this book without help.) Proceed to the Bibleman Web site by typing bibleman.com in your browser window. There, at bibleman.com, you will find easy instructions to obtain your certificate!*